l۱ㄱ

FASTER-THAN-LIGHT
SPACE TRAVEL

BY HOLLY DUHIG

SPACE ROO
volume

THE
SECRET
BOOK
COMPANY

THE SECRET BOOK COMPANY

©2018
**The Secret Book
Company
King's Lynn
Norfolk PE30 4LS**

ISBN: 978-1-912171-07-1

Written by:
Holly Duhig

Edited by:
John Wood

Designed by:
Matt Rumbelow

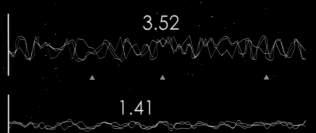

3.52

1.41

SYSTEM
PROTECTION

CONTENTS

Words that appear like this can be found in the glossary on page 31.

FASTER-THAN-LIGHT: THE FANTASY

You're the captain of the fastest spacecraft in the galaxy; but you and your crew need to get to a faraway planet right away! What do you do? Power the engines! Engage the main thrusters! And for goodness' sake put your seatbelt on, because you're about to zoom through space, faster than light itself!

But wait, could this actually be possible in real life? It happens all the time in films and books. You might have heard it called **warp** speed, or hyperspace travel. The idea is that we can cover enormous distances by travelling quicker than the fastest thing in the universe: light.

SCI-FI SPACECRAFT

Imagine if, just like in Star Wars, all it took was the press of a button for your spacecraft to reach incredible speeds. The stars would hurtle past in a blur. In science fiction, spacecraft come in all shapes and sizes. The Doctor's spacecraft looks like a police box and travels by disappearing and reappearing somewhere else.

POLICE PUBLIC CALL BOX

POLICE PUBLIC CALL BOX

Science fiction spaceships might even go into warp gates, which propel them through space really fast. Then they reappear at another warp gate in a completely different star system. But all of this seems like a lot of effort, right? Why would anyone need to go so fast?

THE UNIVERSE IS BIG

It is hard to understand just how big the universe is. There is a lot more space between planets and stars than you think. Venus is usually the closest planet to Earth, but even at its closest point, Venus is still around 38 million kilometres away. To give you an idea of how far that really is, Earth's equator is only 40,075 kilometres around.

VENUS

PROXIMA CENTAURI

Now, imagine we don't want to go to the nearest planet. Instead we want to go to the nearest star to our Sun. That would be the collection of stars known as Alpha Centauri. The smallest star in that collection is called Proxima Centauri, and it is 39,900,000,000,000 kilometres away. It's hard to imagine a distance that long!

PROXIMA CENTAURI IS A RED DWARF STAR. IT IS MUCH SMALLER AND DIMMER THAN OUR SUN, WHICH IS A YELLOW DWARF STAR.

LIGHTYEARS

Now you can see why spaceships have to travel so fast in books and films. If spaceships travelled at normal speeds, it would take hundreds of years to visit nearby planets and stars, let alone the other side of the galaxy.

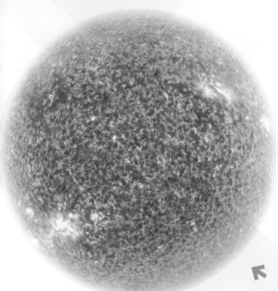

Clearly, space is too big to be measured in kilometres. When scientists measure how far away something is in space, they use a different measurement called a lightyear. A lightyear is based on the distance light can travel in a year which is 9.5 trillion kilometers. If a star was three lightyears away, it would take you three years to get there if you were going at the speed of light. But why do we measure things like this? What is so important about light?

IF YOU WERE WONDERING, PROXIMA CENTAURI IS 4.24 LIGHTYEARS AWAY FROM EARTH. THAT'S A MUCH EASIER NUMBER TO REMEMBER, ISN'T IT?

WHAT IS LIGHT?

Light is a wave of energy, speeding through the universe. It is made up of a bunch of particles travelling along in a row. These particles are called photons. Unlike sound, light can travel through the vacuum of space.

This is all very well and good, but what does it have to do with space travel? Well, there are a few other important things about light. Firstly, unlike most particles, photons have no mass. Secondly, unlike most things, light always travels at the same speed when moving through a vacuum, which is why we measure things in lightyears. These facts are an important part of Albert Einstein's work. Do you know who Einstein is? Well, let's meet him.

TAKE IT AWAY, EINSTEIN

Albert Einstein came up with his **theory** of relativity to explain all the strange things that other scientists couldn't explain. For example: usually the speed of an object looks different depending on the speed we are going ourselves. You can see this happen all the time. If a car drives past you when you're standing still, it looks like it's going really fast. But if you are in your own car, driving alongside at the same speed, the other car doesn't look so fast. It's all **relative**. But this isn't the case with light. Light is always the same speed.

When studying this, Albert Einstein came up with his theories of relativity. They are quite complicated, so here are the only bits that we need to remember right now:

1: NOTHING CAN MOVE FASTER THAN LIGHT.

2: UNLIKE MOST THINGS, LIGHT MOVES AT THE SAME SPEED THROUGH A VACUUM, NO MATTER WHAT SPEED YOU ARE GOING WHEN YOU MEASURE IT.

3: SPACE AND TIME ARE CONNECTED, AND THEY CAN BE BENT AND CHANGED.

4: MASS AND ENERGY ARE THE SAME THING.

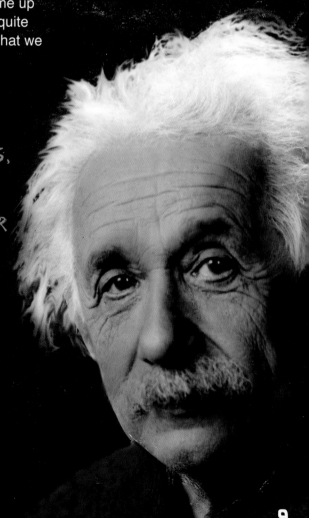

WE MUST GO FASTER

So what is the fastest thing humans have ever built? The Juno spacecraft reached a speed of around 265,000 kilometres per hour when it swung by Jupiter. That's pretty quick. How fast is light, you ask? It is around 300,000 kilometres per second. Wait, per second? Oh dear, we've got a long way to go...

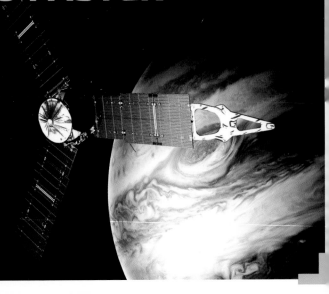

But spacecraft aren't the only fast things humans have built. Deep underground in Switzerland, scientists use the **Large Hadron Collider** to fire tiny particles at each other at incredible speeds. They've managed to fire them at just under the speed of light. I know what you're thinking: just under is no good! We need to go faster than light!

SPEED NEEDS ENERGY

The scientists at the Large Hadron Collider have a problem. The faster an object goes, the more energy is needed to power it. But the energy you use adds to the mass of the object, making it harder to move. This is because mass and energy are the same thing, like Einstein said.

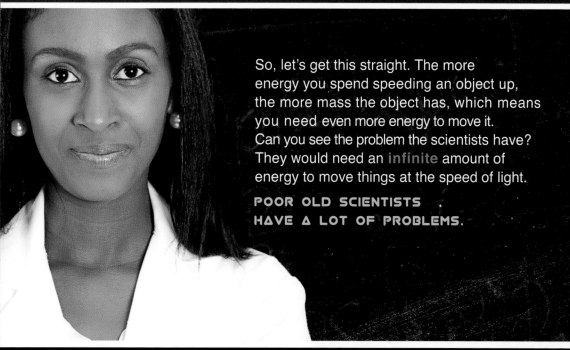

So, let's get this straight. The more energy you spend speeding an object up, the more mass the object has, which means you need even more energy to move it. Can you see the problem the scientists have? They would need an **infinite** amount of energy to move things at the speed of light.

POOR OLD SCIENTISTS HAVE A LOT OF PROBLEMS.

As we know, photons have no mass. This means they don't have to worry about the infinite energy problem. Light is able to travel at its top speed straight away. This is bad news for our spacecraft which does have mass. The fact is we just can't compete with light. It's impossible.

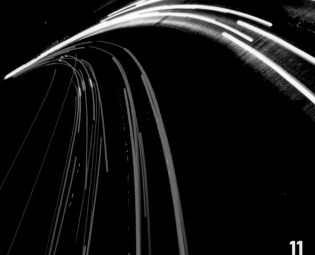

LOADING

FASTER-THAN-LIGHT: THE REALITY

Don't look so down, Captain! You and your crew might still be able to travel the galaxy faster than light.

There may be another way. We just might have to cheat a little.

THE CHERENKOV EFFECT

Light moves at 75% of its normal speed in water. Scientists noticed a bright blue glow around nuclear reactors surrounded by water. This glow is called Cherenkov radiation and is named after the man who studied it, Pavel Cherenkov. It is caused when particles move through the water quicker than light. When this happens, waves of light build up around the particles, because the light isn't going quick enough to get out of the way. This eventually causes a burst of light radiation that looks like a blue glow to us. Of course, space is a vacuum and not full of water, so this won't help us achieve our dreams of space travel.

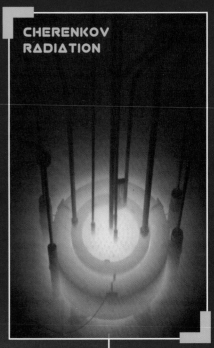

CHERENKOV RADIATION

The same thing happens with sound too. When something goes faster than sound, there is a loud bang as the sound waves build up at the front of the object. It is called a sonic boom.

SHADOWS

Have you ever made shadow puppets with your hands? When you put your hands in front of a light, you can make big shadows on the opposite wall. If you move your fingers just a little bit, the big shadow of your hand also moves. Imagine your light was really powerful, and instead of making shadows on the wall, you made shadows on the clouds in the sky! If you moved your hand, you could make the shadow move miles and miles across the sky in a blink of an eye. Would this shadow be traveling faster than light? Well, not quite. This isn't really the same thing. Even though it looks to us as if the shadow has just moved at high speeds, the shadow is not an object, but rather just a part of the sky that isn't being lit up. So that doesn't help either.

84%

UNIT **11**
complex 7-1-981x

STATUS: SYSTEM OK

CHANGE SETTINGS

4 CORE
142
107
145
183

QUANTUM ENTANGLEMENT

QUANTUM MECHANICS

Scientists are working on something called quantum mechanics. Quantum mechanics is very complicated, but all you have to know is that it is the study of the smallest particles in the universe. When scientists look at really small things like photons, they discover that things can behave very strangely.

Why does light act so strangely? This is the kind of question that quantum mechanics wants to answer.

For example, when scientists measure the properties of a particle they sometimes find that they are exactly the same as another particle that is really far away.

SCIENTISTS ARE STILL WORKING ON QUANTUM MECHANICS. THERE'S STILL A LOT WE DON'T KNOW.

WAVE

PARTICLE

QUANTUM ENTANGLEMENT

Sometimes two particles can become linked by something called quantum entanglement. This sounds very scientific but it basically means that two particles are affecting each other even when they are separated. You could put two entangled particles at opposite ends of the galaxy and they would still affect each other. They are like twins with a **psychic** connection! It's as if one particle knows hat's happening to the other. Scientists still don't know how they communicate so fast! Could we say they it happened faster than light?

Actually, captain, I'm sorry to disappoint you again, but this doesn't really count either. Even though these entangled particles have seemingly communicated faster than the speed of light, no messages have actually been sent across space on some kind of intergalactic highway. But hold on. There is one more idea to explore, and this one just might work.

SYSTEMS OK

84%

GALAXY

LET'S TALK ABOUT SPACE AND TIME

THE BIG BANG THEORY

You might have heard about something called the Big Bang. This is a theory that everything in the universe was once squashed together in one tiny point which then exploded outwards to form all the planets and stars that we can see today. Scientists think that the universe expanded faster than the speed of light just after the Big Bang.

It may be hard to understand, but space and time are not fixed. They can be stretched and squashed. Imagine the universe is like a balloon. After the Big Bang, Space expanded just like the surface of the balloon expands. Now imagine you poke the balloon. Notice how the surface bends around your finger. Well, space and time can be bent in the same way.

A SHORTCUT THROUGH SPACE

Now we are getting somewhere. By bending space, we might be able to go to faraway places faster than light could. We wouldn't be going faster than light; we would just be taking a shortcut. It would be like a race against the fastest kid at school. You both have to get to the finish line but you discover a quicker route. Now, even if you're a much slower runner, you will still win the race!

So, it looks like taking a shortcut through space is the best way forward. It turns out there are a few ways this might be possible. Let's have a look at what they might be.

THE BIG BANG HAPPENED AROUND 14 BILLION YEARS AGO. THE UNIVERSE IS STILL EXPANDING TODAY.

4 CORE

142
107
145
183

SHORTCUT

WORMHOLES
FOLDING SPACE

Here's an activity you can do to understand how wormholes work. All you'll need is a piece of paper and a pencil.

Draw a circle at one end of the paper. This is planet Earth. Now draw a circle at the opposite end of the paper. This is an alien planet that we want to get to. Go ahead and colour them in if you want! It is a long way between the two because they are on opposite ends of the paper. Now flip the paper over and fold it in half. Using your pencil, carefully poke a hole through the folded paper, starting at Earth. There should now be a hole connecting the two planets.

This is what a wormhole is. The idea is you bend space until two separate points that were far away are now touching each other. Then you just need to create a hole and a bridge to cover the small gap. The only problem is how to do this. You would need some way of creating this shortcut and keeping it open. Some scientists believe something called exotic matter might help.

WE WOULD NEED A BRIDGE TO CONNECT THE TWO POINTS IN SPACE.

QUANTUM WORMHOLES

Wormholes might be our best bet for faster-than-light-space travel. Scientists like John Wheeler think that tiny wormholes are created all the time in something called **quantum foam**. Wheeler believes that space is like the sea: when you look at it from the window of an aeroplane it looks smooth and calm but up close it's rough and stormy. He thinks that if we looked at space close up, we would see tiny particles creating wormholes all the time.

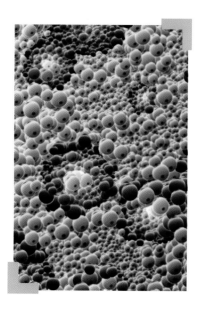

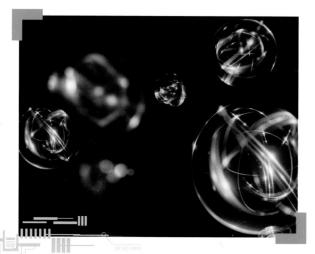

Remember, not a lot is known about our universe and there is still a lot to work out. Perhaps these tiny wormholes wouldn't behave as we expect. Scientists just don't know for sure yet.

These tiny wormholes would also need some of that exotic matter to make them much bigger and stable. I don't suppose you have any, captain? Check your pockets. No? Oh well.

BLACK HOLES AND WHITE HOLES

BLACK HOLES

We need to make sure we know what a black hole is. Black holes are points in space which suck up anything that comes near them. The force of a black hole is so strong that it warps time and space around it. Not even light can escape the clutches of a black hole. A black hole has an invisible area around it, called an event horizon. Only things that cross that event horizon are sucked in.

If you looked at a black hole, you wouldn't be able to see it. However, if any matter was about to fall in the event horizon, you may be able to see that.

But just because you can't see them, doesn't mean they are empty. Quite the opposite! Black holes squash lots of matter into a tiny **singularity**. The amount of matter that a black hole contains depends on the size. A black hole the size of an **atom** might hold as much mass as a mountain.

WHITE HOLES

Unlike black holes, white holes have never been seen in the universe. They only exist in theory. White holes are time-reversed black holes which act in the opposite way. They don't suck things up, they spit them out!

THIS IS WHAT A WHITE HOLE MIGHT LOOK LIKE IF WE SAW ONE.

Behind every black hole there may be a wormhole leading to a white hole. If this is the case, we could use a black hole as a shortcut to travel faster than light. Of course, nobody knows for sure. Maybe you should jump into a black hole and find out? You'll either appear on the other side of a white hole or be instantly crushed into a singularity. On second thoughts, captain, that sounds like a terrible idea. Let's wait for the scientists to work it out, instead.

ONLINE STATISTIC

PROFILE 7553-2V

OBJECT: C-34/25
STATUS: SYSTEM OK
MODE: STEADY
CHANGE SETTINGS ▫

WARP DRIVES

We've looked at bending space like a piece of paper, but what about stretching and squashing it? Well, here is the theory of the warp drive. A man called Miguel Alcubierre came up with the idea, and many scientists have added to his theory since. Just a little warning, this method also needs some of that exotic matter. Actually, this method needs a lot of that exotic matter.

WARPING SPACE INTO A WAVE

The idea is the exotic matter would bend space into a wave shape, meaning the space in front would become small and squished, while the space behind would become big and inflated. All this time our spaceship would be sitting still in a bubble of normal space in the middle. This bubble would ride the warped wave across the galaxies faster than the speed of light.

PROBLEMS WITH THE WARP DRIVE

There are still a few things we need to work out before this is possible in any way. One problem is that we have no idea how to stop this wave when we need to get off. We'd be trapped forever in our bubble of normal space, like an intergalactic hamster in a ball.

> BEING A HAMSTER IN A BALL ISN'T AS FUN WHEN YOU'RE GOING FASTER-THAN-LIGHT.

DON'T FORGET ABOUT EXOTIC MATTER!

The other problem is you would need an enormous amount of exotic matter to power this warp drive, especially if you were going long distances (which is kind of the point of faster-than-light space travel). In fact, it has been suggested that it isn't possible to have enough energy in the same place at the same time to power a warp drive. But we don't know this for sure. We certainly can't rule this kind of space travel out yet.

EXOTIC MATTER

WHAT DO WE MEAN BY EXOTIC MATTER?

When we talk about exotic matter, we are talking about something called negative mass.

But what is negative mass? Well, it helps to think of it like electricity. Electric **charge** can be positive or negative. This is why there are positive and negative ends on batteries. Scientists think that – just like an electric charge – mass can also be positive and negative. All the things we see around us have a positive mass. If something had negative mass, however, it would behave differently to everything else. It would act in the opposite way. That means if you pushed an object that was made of negative mass, it would move towards you. How strange!

FUEL FOR THE WARP DRIVE

A warp drive needs negative mass in order to work. Black holes have positive mass so they squash space and suck everything in. Negative mass would do the exact opposite. It would cause space to expand. It could even be used to create a wave in space big enough to make a faster-than-light-warp drive.

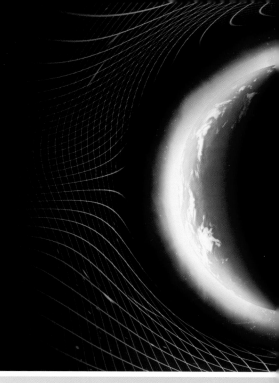

WHERE IS IT HIDING?

So, when can we get some of this stuff? Well that's the problem. We can't. Not yet. Scientists believe this stuff exists but haven't been able to find it anywhere in the universe.

37

Rb

FASTER-THAN-LIGHT: THE FUTURE

It looks like the scientists still have a bit more work to do. But what if all of this was possible right now? Well, faster-than-light travel would mean we could travel outside of our solar system, to distant stars and planets across our galaxy. We think there are over a billion Earth-like planets that could support life in our galaxy. If there are aliens out there, and if we want to talk to them, we will need to move through space a lot faster.

ESCAPE PLAN

But there's another reason to travel to these Earth-like planets. Our planet is amazing but it might not be around forever. What if an asteroid hits our planet? What about when our Sun dies and stops making light and heat? There are lots of reasons we might have to leave Earth, and it sure would be useful to have another nice, Earth-like planet to go to.

DON'T WORRY, IT'LL PROBABLY BE OVER A MILLION YEARS BEFORE AN ASTEROID HITS OUR PLANET, AND BILLIONS OF YEARS BEFORE THE SUN DIES. BUT STILL, IT IS GOOD TO PLAN AHEAD, RIGHT?

3.52

1.41

A SPIRAL GALAXY

It might be nice to go to a different galaxy altogether. There are lots of different galaxies in our universe. Our galaxy, the Milky Way, is a big **spiral galaxy**. There are also lots of dwarf galaxies. But if we want to visit these, we will definitely need faster-than-light-travel.

GOODBYE GALAXIES

For reasons scientists aren't quite sure about, most galaxies are actually speeding away from each other, faster and faster. You would think they would be slowing down after the explosive Big Bang, but this is not the case. As we know, space can expand faster than light travels. If these galaxies keep speeding up, even the most advanced spaceships won't be fast enough to catch up with them.

THE ANDROMEDA GALAXY IS THE NEAREST SPIRAL GALAXY TO OUR OWN AT 2.5 MILLION LIGHTYEARS AWAY. IT IS MOVING TOWARDS US AND IN 4.5 BILLION YEARS WE WILL COLLIDE.

THE MILKY WAY

PROFILE 7553-2V
OBJECT: C-34/25
STATUS: SYSTEM OK
MODE: STEADY
CHANGE SETTINGS ►

TIME TRAVEL

In the future of faster-than-light travel, there is something else we have to think about. According to Einstein's theory of relativity, the closer to the speed of light you travel, the slower time will be for you. This is called time dilation. This means it would be possible for you to go on a trip that only took you two years but 30 years would have passed for your friends and family back on Earth. You would have traveled into the future.

The difference in time between you and Earth depends on how fast and how far you go. If we ever learn how to travel near the speed of light, we'll need to keep this in mind.

IT LOOKS LIKE TRAVELLING TO THE FUTURE IS A LOT EASIER THAN TRAVELLING TO THE PAST.

SYSTEM PROTECTION

LOGIN
PASSWORD

WHAT ARE SCIENTISTS WORKING ON RIGHT NOW?

In reality we have a long way to go before we travel faster than light. At the moment, scientists all over the world are concentrating on other things, such as building rockets that can get us to Mars. The point is, the scientists have lots to do, but faster-than-light space travel probably isn't at the top of their list.

LANDING ON MARS IS ONE OF OUR NEXT BIG MISSIONS

Anyway, for now we have our own solar system to learn about. There is plenty to explore, like Saturn's moons, the surface of Mars and the outer planets like Neptune and Uranus. Who knows what space travel will be like in the future? Perhaps going faster than light isn't as far off as we think.

ONLINE STATISTIC

PROFILE 7553-2V

OBJECT: C-34/25
STATUS: SYSTEM OK
MODE: STEADY
CHANGE SETTINGS

1.592
1.586
1.572
1.561
1.554
1.541
1.532

WHERE WOULD YOU GO?

The universe is full of strange, wonderful things. If you could travel faster-than-light, you could explore it all. So, where would you go? Would you go to HD 189733b, a planet where it rains shards of molten glass? Would you go to VY Canis Majoris, one of the biggest stars we know about, 2,600 times the size of the Sun?

Perhaps you would go to The Great Attractor, an enormous, mysterious thing that is pulling whole galaxies towards it. Or would you head outside the observable universe, beyond everything we've ever seen before? Would you keep the main thrusters on until you reach the very edge? Is there an edge?

WE HAVE A LOT OF QUESTIONS, SO IF YOU EVER DO TRAVEL ACROSS THE GALAXY MAKE SURE YOU SEND EARTH A POSTCARD. REMEMBER TO SEND IT FASTER-THAN-LIGHT THOUGH, OTHERWISE IT IS GOING TO TAKE FOREVER TO REACH US.

GLOSSARY

asteroid	rocky and irregularly shaped objects that orbit around the Sun
atom	the smallest part of a chemical element, which is made up of even smaller particles.
charge	an amount of electric energy, which can either be positive or negative depending on if there are more or less negative electrons around
energy	the power required for an activity
exotic matter	a theoretical combination of positive and negative mass that would be used in faster-than-light space travel
infinite	endless
mass	the amount of matter that a body or object contains
nuclear reactors	device which splits atoms using nuclear fission to produce energy and nuclear material
Large Hadron Collider	a machine that uses magnets to fire particles around a huge ring near the speed of light.
observable universe	the parts of the universe we can see because its light has had time to reach us
photons	the smallest particle of light, which has wave-like properties and no mass
properties	physical qualities of something
psychic	spiritual, supernatural or 'magical' powers, especially to do with the mind
quantum foam	the idea that the very fabric of the universe is rough and changing when you look at it extremely close up
radiation	the release of energy as waves or particles
relative	considered in relation or proportion to something else
singularity	a point in space where matter is squashed into a single point, which is usually the centre of a black hole
spiral galaxy	galaxies where the stars, dust and gas form winding, spiral arms that branch out from the centre
theory	an explanation of how something works based on facts that have been tested
vacuum	a space devoid of matter
warp	to bend into a different shape

INDEX

Photocredits: Abbreviations: l-left, r-right, b-bottom, t-top, c-centre, m-middle. Images courtesy of Shutterstock.com. With thanks to Getty Images, Thinkstock Photo and iStockphoto. Cover: bg – MaxyM; front – Halfpoint. 2 – tsuneomp. 4/5 – DM7. 5: bg – Aperture75; tr – Graeme Dawes. 6: tr – Vadim Sadovski. Bl – Igor Kovalchuk. 7: t – DM7; br – DM7. 8 – ixpert. 9: t – hxdyl; b – Rocket Rider; br – Orren Jack Turner/Library of Congress/Wikipedia, 10: t – Vadim Sadovski; bl – Maximilien Brice, CERN / CERN Document Server. 11: m – pathdoc-mixed; b – RexRover. 12: bg – Daniel Prudek; mr – United States Nuclear Regulatory Commission. 13: t – Anatoliy Lukich; b – Copacabana. 14: m – agsandrew; bl – Mr.Moon; br – agsandrew. 15 – Aphelleon. 16 – Mix_universe-balloon. 17: bg – Annette Shaff; tr – Vadim Sadovski; b – Kaspri. 18: t – FabrikaSimf. B – Interior Design. 19: t – GiroScience; m – Dmitriy Rybin; b – GiroScience. 20 – Vadim Sadovski. 21: bg – paulista; ml – tsuneomp. 22: t – tsuneomp; b – Paraksa. 23: t – Africa Studio. B – BarGar. 24: t – Somchai Som; ml – TW Stocker; mc – Kotkot32; mr – Avesun. b – wacomka. 25 – graysolid. 26 – Igor Zh. 27: tl – Vadim Sadovski; b – Fabio Lamanna. 28 – underworld. 29: tr – Sergey Nivens; b – Alones. 30: bg – Romolo Tavani; bl – tsuneomp; tr – vs148.